Cont...

G000152708

The Ramblers' Association promotes country walking, protects rights of way, campaigns for access to open country, woodlands etc. and defends the beauty of the landscape. The RA plays a major role in securing legislation to protect our paths and countryside. Please give your support by becoming a member. Write to: The Ramblers' Association, 2nd Floor, Camelford House, 87-90 Albert Embankment, London SE1 7TW.
Tel 020 7339 8500. **Fax** 020 7339 8501.
email ramblers@london.ramblers.org.uk   **website** www.ramblers.org.uk

Berkshire Area
The RA has seven groups across the county, each of which arranges its own programme of walks and other events. For details of the individual groups contact John Moules, 50 Qualitas, Roman Hill, Bracknell, Berkshire RG12 7QG.

Cookhamdean Common and Bisham Woods

A few well-farmed fields, lots of wild woods, a couple of inviting pubs; mainly on the high ground overlooking the Thames Valley above historic Bisham. An opportunity to enjoy part of the 67 square miles of woodland across the country, where public access and sensitive management is assured by the Woodland Trust.

Distance: 6½ miles
OS Map: Explorer 172 Chiltern Hills East
Start: Cookham Station
(Grid ref: 887 851)

From station forecourt walk over level crossing, turn left through car park, to join High Road and shortly to turn left along Peace Lane, then Shergold Way to enter playing field. Bear right up middle of field, past corner of allotments, to exit at gap about half-way along top boundary. Cross garage area and follow estate roads round left and right bends until, just before T-junction ahead, turn left beside green strip, then carefully cross road ahead into Lesters Road. Shortly turn left and find tarmac pathway between Lesters Cottages. Swing-gate leads to path between fences which shortly crosses wide gravel track and goes straight ahead between fields, to emerge at road (Long Lane).

1 Turn right up road, using verge where possible. At top of field on left (pausing to admire view towards Windsor Castle) turn left on grass path beside hedge. Bear right into next field, still with hedge on right until, when level with metal gates, turn half-left across field. At corner of wood ahead (Beeching Grove Wood) continue to corner of field and on between trees. Facing open field ahead, turn right, with hedge on right. About half-way along *second* side of this field *turn sharp right* on woodland path. Reaching corner of property ahead bear right on winding path to end of woodland, opposite house known as Butlers Gate.

2 Keep to verge on right into Choke Lane before crossing to NT sign and into wide track. At open common, bear left on worn path along left side of common, with road nearby on left until,

Marlow and the Thames from Quarry Woods

a few yards before parking area, turn left through gap in hedge to cross road into wide track. Follow this past buildings of Park Farm. Shortly after large property at beginning of woods ahead, turn right through gap beside wooden gate, engraved Woodland Trust ('Walkers are welcome to walk in our woods'). This is Inkydown Wood, the beginning for us of a 1½ mile sweep through Bisham Woods.

3 Keep left at next two forks ahead, now sloping down, soon with fine views over Thames-side Bisham village and towards Chiltern Hills. Keep to main path as it descends, increasingly steeply, finally down to major path junction in deep gulley. Here turn half-right up stony bridleway, shortly keeping left at first fork. Before top of gulley, fork left onto footpath, to climb more steeply. After some distance, the footpath bears left (at white waymark arrow) and continues along edge of ridge, dropping to road. With great care walk up road for 50 yards, then cross over and take narrow path, close to

road at first. Stay on this mainly level path to emerge on drive to 'Rivendell' and, just ahead through bushes, the viewpoint on Winter Hill.

4 Having savoured the view (and perhaps an ice cream!), turn right, back along road past Dial Place, before turning left down a byway - Job's Lane. Cross lane into sunken footpath and after another crossing lane go straight up the common ahead, shortly bearing left up a chalky track leading to, and then beside, the Green at Cookham Dean. (To catch a train from Cookham allow 30 minutes from here.)

5 At War Memorial turn right along Church Road and then left on track beside church and burial ground. Continue down drive (a public path), passing Huntsmans Cottage. After swing-gate join fenced path, known as Kennel Lane, towards distant roofs of Cookham. At bottom of track go ahead into High Road, leading back into this delightful village and to station at start.

DATE WALKED		

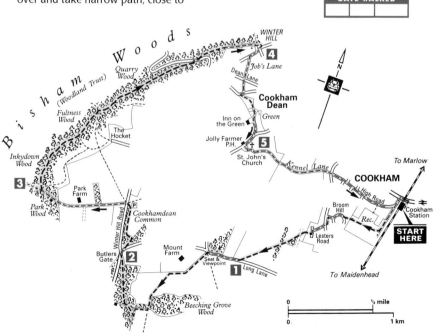

Maidenhead Thicket and Pinkney's Green

Enjoy the freedom to roam over the 850 acres of commons and greens, once part of the Saxon Royal Manor of Cookham, now in the safe keeping of the National Trust. Highwaymen are rare today in the Thicket but there is wildlife a-plenty in its leafy glades.

Distance: 5½ miles
OS Map: Explorer 172 Chiltern Hills East
Start: National Trust parking area off Cannon Lane, Maidenhead. (Grid ref: 859 803) See map for alternative start at Furze Platt School.

Facing NT sign take left-hand path (of three) along the broad grass ride ahead, with boundary hedge of Maidenhead Thicket on left. Where main ride swings right, keep straight on along narrow path passing buildings on left (Clare Court School). Cross tarmac drive and descend steps (cut in 1975 by scouts of Maidenhead Boyne Hill troop) and along path through old chalkpit to swing-gate and turn right along road (Cherry Garden Lane). The first of several Maidenhead boundary stones on this walk is just ahead, outside Heathside Cottage, corner property on left.

1 Go ahead along lane and just before main road (A4) bear right, cutting across grass strip to use traffic-island over road, then follow footpath ahead into Maidenhead Thicket. At prominent crossing ride, bear right along it to a point 25 yards beyond first waymark post, then bear left on path into trees. Soon cross avenue of mature trees and carry on to end of Thicket woodland. Just ahead descend slope and go under road bridge before bearing right up slope and along a ridged path to road. Another stone is on nearside verge to left here.

2 Cross road into broad grass ride ahead. *You may like to add a short detour (few minutes each way) to view the*

attractively situated Stubbings Church, by taking the gated path on left just before first house ahead. Try to spot the next boundary stone tucked away just right of wooden gate of Leigh Cottage. Now continue along roadway (Darling's Lane) to a junction. On the island here used to be a damaged Boundary Stone; can you find it?

3 Continue ahead for some 85 yards and look for another stone on left, just beyond entrance of Greenlands. Pass last house, St Timothee's, and shortly ahead follow edge of Pinkney's Green, then gravel drive. At road ahead turn left for about 60 yards, then left again, to find another stone, by start of footpath, plus two 'boundary nails' embedded in nearby oak tree. Return to road, cross to Golden Ball Lane and fork left along gravel track past Fairwinds. After wooden rails fork right beside wooded NT common. Reaching cottage on right go straight ahead across green and road to enter Malders Lane.

Follow lane, noticing NT Brick & Tile Works on right. At buildings of Hindhay Farm turn right, across concrete yard in front of farmhouse, to go through swing-gate ahead, fenced at first, then widening to mid-field path. On far side of field, after swing-gate, turn right behind buildings (Littlewick Farm) and follow drive. Where boarded fence on right stops, turn right beside it and after a few yards aim half-left across field, to cross the road by '40' speed sign.

4 Stay near road along edge of common ahead at first, then bear right, beside line of bushes on left. Pass to right of large chestnut tree and nearby cricket green. Shortly after end of trees on left, bear right across open common, aiming just right of white(ish) house (beside tall chestnut tree) on far side into Bix Lane. Cross green to road ahead and back onto common, keeping road nearby on left. Reaching

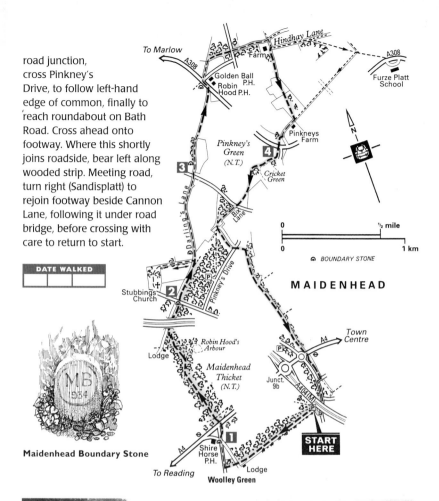

road junction, cross Pinkney's Drive, to follow left-hand edge of common, finally to reach roundabout on Bath Road. Cross ahead onto footway. Where this shortly joins roadside, bear left along wooded strip. Meeting road, turn right (Sandisplatt) to rejoin footway beside Cannon Lane, following it under road bridge, before crossing with care to return to start.

To Marlow

Hindhay Lane

Farm

To Marlow

A308

Golden Ball P.H.
Robin Hood P.H.

Furze Platt School

A308

Pinkneys Farm

Pinkney's Green (N.T.)

3

4

Cricket Green

Darling's Lane

Bix Lane

MAIDENHEAD

0   ½ mile

0   1 km

◉ BOUNDARY STONE

Stubbings Church

2

P

Pinkney's Drive

Robin Hood's Arbour

Lodge

Maidenhead Thicket (N.T.)

Town Centre

A4

P

Junct. 9b

A404(M)

START HERE

A4

Shire Horse P.H.

1

Lodge

To Reading

Woolley Green

DATE WALKED

MB 1934

Maidenhead Boundary Stone

This green was acquired by public subscription in 1934

Woolley Green and Shottesbrooke

Whilst a sea of 20th-century development now laps up close to one of Berkshire's most historic houses, the 15th-century Ockwells Manor, it still provides a peaceful start and finish to this walk. But the high spot for many will be the medieval church at Shottesbrooke, in its splendid parkland setting.

Distance: 7½ miles

OS Map: Explorer 160 Windsor

Start: Ockwells Road, by Ockwells Manor, near Cox Green, Maidenhead.
(Grid ref: 875 789)

With your back to Ockwells Manor entrance gates turn left and walk to end of this quiet lane. Here cross over, turning right, then left at mini-roundabout into Highfield Lane. If you want to know how long it takes to walk exactly one kilometre, check your watch now, then look again when you reach the end of this road at Cannon Lane.

1 Take turning to right of the (Thatched Cottage) pub into Firs Lane which soon narrows, becoming a field-path with hedge on left. At end of field go straight on, soon through woodland strip. At end of trees cross stile and go half-left over small field to leave beside gate. Join concrete track ahead to road, the hamlet of Woolley Green, one of several local Greens once in Windsor Forest.

Turn left along lane until, opposite large colour-washed house, turn right up bank. Field path ahead soon crosses road (to Business Park) and continues as wide farm track with views over hedge on right to Ashley Hill (474 ft.) and on left to distant spire of our objective, Shottesbrooke Church. At T-junction of tracks, turn left and where this soon forks, keep right for 100 yards, then bear left on mid-field line, aiming just right of distant barn. *Overhead the sound of light aircraft from White Waltham flying club often competes with the skylarks!*

Follow the drive past Shottesbrooke House ...

2 On far side of field, facing hedge, turn right to road, then left over bridge, passing Shottesbrooke Farm. Straight stretch of lane soon reveals flint-built lodge. Turn right here along drive and, where trees end, the path line bears left on grass, to join tarmac drive passing in front of house to reach the splendid church of St John, inspired by Salisbury Cathedral and unaltered since its completion in 1337.

3 From church kissing-gate, follow line of path from stone waymarker, across park left of pond (sometimes dry). After stile on far side, path narrows through wooded strip (notice badger sett) and emerges at cricket field. Unless visiting 'Beehive' ahead, turn right, round edge of field, pass behind pavilion and cross road into Walgrove Gardens. Keep left of green, then pass right of house ahead and over stile. Keep left of first field, then along right side of field above, to turn right along lane in front of Waltham Place.

Follow lane (Church Hill) passing fountain commemorating 60 years of Queen Victoria's reign. At junction (B3024) go ahead for 100 yards and turn left through swing-gate to follow left side of two fields. Entering third field turn left, still beside wood. In field corner turn right, looking for point where path dips down over culvert on left into wooded strip. Emerging in field ahead, turn left for 15 yards, then go through swing-gate and along right-hand field-edge, soon joining wide track (Snowball Hill).

4 Turn right at junction and pass buildings of Heywood Farm. By first house on right, turn right along field-edge until, at start of trees, turn right along wooden walk-way. In field ahead, follow ditch at first, heading towards distant buildings (Ockwells Manor). Eventually, at end of field, cross stile by pair of gates and bear left along unmade Thrift Lane, leading back to start.

DATE WALKED		

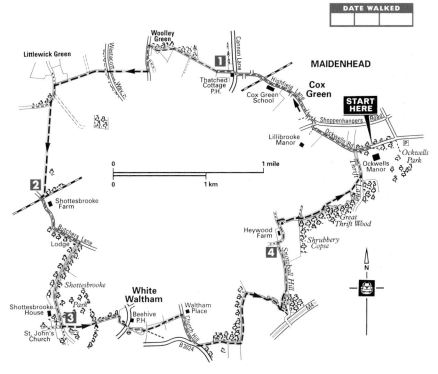

Littlewick Green and Prospect Hill

Sample two of East Berkshire's unspoilt villages and climb the quiet woodland path to enjoy the panoramic view from Prospect Hill, overlooking the Thames at Hurley to the Buckinghamshire Chilterns.

Distance: 5 miles
OS Map: Explorer 172 Chiltern Hills East
Start: Burchett's Green Primary School, Burchett's Green Lane. (Grid ref: 838 812)

With your back to the road head across parking area beside school and onto woodland path over common. Emerging at roadside turn right. (Looking back along road here you can see Stubbings Manor with its unusual 'dove tower'.) Look for bridleway forking right off lane, opposite Old Oak Farm. Appropriately called Green Lane with view of Ashley Hill on right, it leads to the Bath Road (A4). Just before main road, cut across corner of common on left, so as cross road via traffic-island. Go ahead into Jubilee Road and at beginning of Green turn right along track to pass pavilion, with sundial inscribed:

*'Tis mine the passing hours to tell
'Tis thine to use them ill or well!*

1 Turn right along road ahead for some 60 yards, then opposite April Cottage turn left into narrow fenced path. Path goes straight ahead along field-edge, then beside track, before passing buildings of Frogmore Farm. Continue ahead across open field to stile in hedge on far side. The path line here continues straight ahead across pub garden. Pass to right of tall car park hedge and over strip of common to re-cross Bath Road at traffic island. Go down steps and turn right along middle of common, soon with field close on left.

2 Cross a gravel drive and bear right on woodland path. Where this almost reaches lay-by for a bus-stop, turn left and join a wide path ahead with thick woodland (Ashley Hill Wood) on either side. We shall be following this, in the same direction, ignoring prominent crossing tracks, for about 1½ miles. At one point, beside wire-fenced reservoir, our path bears slightly right, dips into a hollow, crosses a drive, before finally descending through trees to emerge at lane by Ladyeplace Cottages.

Ashley Hill Wood is part of the Forestry Commission's Chiltern Forest and was leased in 1951. Its 80 hectares (200 acres) was largely re-planted during the fifties with

Hall Place   *Painting by John Manson*

a variety of species, including oak, beech, pine and spruce. The wood was last thinned in 1998 and this is due again in 2008.

3 Cross stile to left of cottages and follow right side of meadow. Ignore ladder stile and at bottom corner of field pass through two metal swing-gates and then on across next field. Cross concrete farm track and head towards distant trees (High Wood). Go straight through this wood leading to the splendid viewpoint on far side, known as Prospect Hill.

Now turn right along edge of woodland (Bisham Church in view half-left). Path turns back into the wood before emerging to dip down across the farmland, heading straight towards the buildings of Hall Place and Farm. Path becomes a track and keeps right of farm buildings before narrowing between fences, to join tree-lined avenue.

4 Reaching front of Hall Place mansion (built 1728-35) turn left onto main drive for a short distance, before forking right where signed footpath runs diagonally across field. After an old kissing-gate continue on grass path, then a metalled drive, leading past a cluster of cottages and old houses to reach the centre of Burchett's Green, opposite the Crown. Bear right along the road, shortly to return to start.

DATE WALKED

PROSPECT HILL

High Wood

Hall Place

4

3 Ladyeplace Cottages

Res

Ashley Hill

Wood

2

Common

Frogmore Farm

Ring O'Bells P.H.

A4 Bath Road

Cricketers P.H.

1

Burchett's Green

Crown P.H.

START HERE

Stubbings Manor

School

Green Lane

Burchetts Green La

To Maidenhead

Littlewick Green

To Reading

N

0   ½ mile

0   1 km

Ashley Hill and Dewdrop Inn

This refreshing walk begins by climbing to the summit of Ashley Hill (474 ft) with fine views back over Berkshire. Visit Brakspear's tucked away Dewdrop Inn, once a simple ale-house, now with a fresh lease of life for the 21st century.

Distance: 3¼ miles
OS Maps: Explorer 159 Reading and 172 Chiltern Hills East
Start: Lay-by near 'Seven Stars' on Bath Road (A4) at Knowl Hill. (Grid ref: 822 794)

With your back to 'Seven Stars' turn left along footway, passing Village Hall. At lay-by beyond last building (one-time village stores) bear left over parking area to road ahead (Warren Row Road). Cross road, pass metal barrier and bear left over strip of common to stile step in metal gate. Here in Bottle Meadow (site of annual Steam Fair) aim up through middle to exit at field-gate in far top corner. From here go ahead up drive for 35 yards, then cross stile on left into field corner.

1 Follow wire fence on right, shortly to cross stile ahead and go uphill with hedgerow on right. In next field continue climbing, now with hedge on left. At top corner cross stile into woodland path, narrow at first, soon becoming wide track, winding up to the top of Ashley Hill. *This is the site of a one-time Victorian keeper's cottage, now sadly over-developed, since being auctioned by the Forestry Commission in 1987.*

From top of hill continue, now on grassy track, which soon turns left quite steeply downhill with views through trees to far horizon. A few yards beyond wooden stileway turn right, along level bridleway. Pass wooden gate and some 50 yards ahead along drive turn left down to Dewdrop Inn.
2 From pub continue down bridleway until, entering field ahead, immediately turn left over footbridge by stile, then left again, to follow the present right of way close to fence line on left. From stile into adjoining field, bear right to another on far side, backed by trees (Channers Wood). At

Loddon Valley RA Group members near Pudding Hill

this point turn left up track for 50 yards, then cross footbridge on right to follow path beside fence ahead, becoming a track between fences.

3 Reaching metal field-gate go ahead a dozen paces before turning left over stile and heading down to another stile in field bottom. Same path-line through paddocks ahead leads to exit just left of property. In front of this house turn left up track for 50 yards then turn right onto path through woodland strip, leading down to roadside. Cross ahead into trees of Lot Wood.

4 On far side of wood cross bridleway and stile. Path ahead is fenced for short distance beside first field. Entering next field ahead, go diagonally across it, aiming left of distant trees, to exit at stile in corner. Turn left for 20 paces, cross stile on right and follow hedge on left. Leave field at swing-gate and a few yards ahead turn left, by charming timber-clad cottage, into top end of Star Lane, to follow ribbon of homesteads downhill towards the mounting rumble of traffic along Bath Road.

As you turn left, to pass immediatly in front of the 'Seven Stars', can you imagine the sights and sounds of the 18th century stagecoaches as they clattered into the forecourt of the 'Seven Stars', to refresh the travellers and change the horses, perhaps after a brush with highwaymen on Maidenhead Thicket?

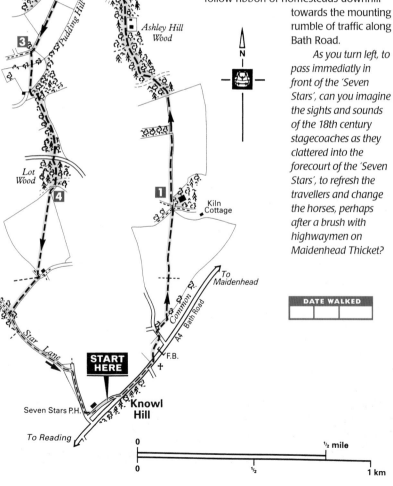

DATE WALKED		

Bowsey Hill and Juddmonte Farm

Hills, woods, meadows, fields and a new (permissive) footpath. Climb to the top of tree-clad Bowsey Hill, a landmark visible for many miles around. Stroll beside peaceful paddocks of an internationally famous stud farm.

Distance: 4½ miles
OS Maps: Explorer 159 Reading and 172 Chiltern Hills East
Start: Lay-by near 'Seven Stars' on Bath Road (A4) at Knowl Hill. (Grid ref: 822 794)

With your back to 'Seven Stars' turn right, cross Star Lane and (biting the bullet and braving the traffic noise) hurry along the short distance beside the A4 until, opposite the 'Old Devil', turn right into the quiet haven of Canhurst Lane! Follow rising right of

Our route beyond Lot Wood

way through an old iron kissing-gate, along a woodland strip to reach a wooden swing-gate.

1 The path straight on has been officially diverted for some years to come to enable mineral working to take place. So turn left along the rough stony track provided as an alternative, soon dipping down. At bottom of gulley the diverted path climbs to right but instead cross wide plank bridge and follow a permissive path meandering through woodland, to emerge at junction with bridleway. Here turn right uphill, soon joining raised, segregated path, beside Lindenhill Wood, a route believed to have Roman origins. At top of climb continue ahead, now on a level segregated path, leading past scattered properties on upper slopes of Bowsey Hill.

2 Path joins descending roadway (Hatchgate Lane), soon with view on right of substantial house, Cayton Park. At crossroad (known as Holly Cross) by lodge, turn right along quiet lane. At next crossroad go straight on into Rose Lane, looking for stile shortly on right. Take this path, soon beside paddock. *The thoroughbred foals often seen grazing here in the early months of each year may be racing on the famous courses of the world three years later. Pick the winners now!*

3 The path turns sharp left along next side of this first paddock, then right, across wide grass strip, passing the immaculate brick and flint buildings of Juddmonte Farm, (formerly Pudders Farm). At end of buildings turn left along tarmac drive until, where this turns left, go straight ahead across grass to stile in corner. Path descends beside hedge to pair of stiles at bottom of slope where we have a choice of ways.

4 For the 'summer route', perhaps, go through gap in fence and turn right along tree-shaded old bridleway, known as Hodgedale Lane. *This was* *once used by local tradesmen driving their traps between Warren Row and the Henley Road.* In winter you may prefer the drier option by turning right along the parallel grass path, to the end of the paddocks, then turning left over stile to join Hodgedale Lane.

Either way, the old lane soon joins a broad farm track, becoming a concrete roadway past cottages. Keep left of grass triangle (signed Pudding Hill) and go straight on along road (facing traffic) and where this swings left, go straight ahead into trees of Lot Wood.

5 Cross stile by footbridge over ditch and turn left along side of meadow to leave over stile in far top corner. Hedged track leads to isolated cottage, in *front* of which turn right over stile and aim for right-hand end of trees ahead. From this point field-path descends diagonally to stile by houses. Join track ahead which soon leads back to start.

Spindle-tree alongside our route

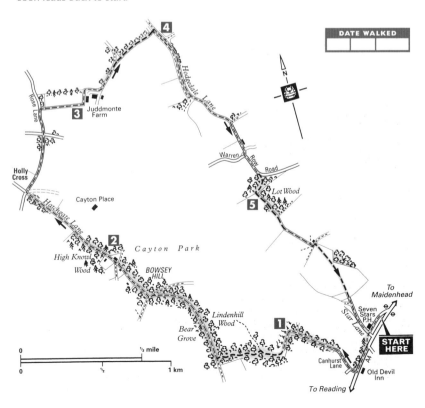

DATE WALKED

High Knowl Wood and Penny's Lane

The hamlet of Crazies Hill has changed little in the last hundred years. The sometimes hilly paths we use today through the small fields and quiet woods still provide the views familiar to the Victorians in 1900 who hauled the materials from nearby Henley-on-Thames, to rebuild the former Georgian Town Hall (of 1795), in its new country setting.

Distance: 4 miles
OS Map: Explorer 171 Chiltern Hills West
Start: North end of Crazies Hill Road by C of E. Primary School.
(Grid ref: 799 808)

With your back to the school turn right along footway. Just past entrance to Summerfield House (the former Town Hall, see above) cross road and turn left beside village hall, keeping left into narrow path, hedged at first. At end of grass path beside paddocks, cross stile and turn right along quiet lane. This soon slopes down and at bottom of dip turn left through gap beside wooden gate and go ahead along path beside wood, soon bearing slightly right between two large trees. Waymarked path (painted arrows) climbs steadily ahead with fir plantation (part of High Knowl Wood) nearby on right.

1 Eventually, path descends to junction. Here go straight on over two crossing tracks as path dips down. Path winds ahead, passes through two stileways (to deter horses?). Improved path surface steadily ascends until, with swing-gate 25 yards ahead and saw mill in sight, turn right, downhill. At one point, notice down through avenue of trees on left a large house known as Yeldhall Manor.

2 Towards bottom of slope, path merges with bed of stream (!) before reaching swing-gate ahead. Now bear right, down side of rough field, before turning right on path into wood, crossing narrow ditch and ahead to footbridge, soon followed by wooden stepped boardwalk. Path levels out, with fir trees in wood on right. At path junction cross stile ahead to descend down mid-field path, across line of oaks, to stile by gate.

Penny's Lane

Turn right along lane as far as end of field (by Highfield Farmhouse), and turn left over stile in corner. Within a few yards bear right onto gravel track. Where this track ends, turns right between wooden posts, to join a wide, curving grass track ahead which climbs over a low hill. Avenue of mature trees leads down to stile by gate. Keep near ditch and copse on right to leave field in corner and continue along edge of garden of bungalow (Penny Green) to emerge at road.

3 Turn right along road for some 30 paces then turn sharp left down bridleway (Penny's Lane). Follow this old sunken track for about ½ mile, bending sharp left at about the half-way point.

4 At end of long field on left, by wooden field-gate, turn right up bank to squeeze-stile and climb fenced path. At top of hill pause to enjoy fine view towards Henley in the river valley and the Chiltern Hills beyond. Keep along top of pasture (with handsome white house in view ahead) before dropping down to leave field at swing-gate. Now bear right, up narrow lane, past Worley's Hill and, shortly, farm of that name too.

5 Follow lane and turn right over stile by first tree in group ahead. Take path through two fields, towards left side of prominent white building (that old Town Hall again!). Path leaves corner of second field over stile, leading to road, close to our starting point.

DATE WALKED		

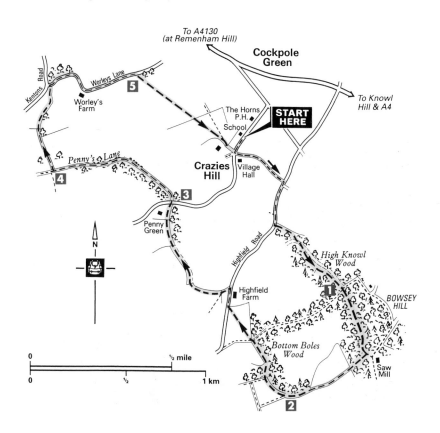

Rebecca's Well and Bottom Boles Wood

An easy climb through fields and tracks to the modest heights of Crazies Hill, a hamlet which seems to have side-stepped the 20th century. From the charmingly decorated Well, saunter along old paths through older woods, finally along a new field-path back into thriving Wargrave.

Distance: 4½ miles

OS Map: Explorer 171 Chiltern Hills West

Start: Recreation Ground, off Victoria Road. Wargrave. (Grid ref: 794 786)

From recreation ground walk back down Recreation Road and turn left down Victoria Road. Notice on left the posh entrance gates of 'Woodclyffe Allotments 1903', before crossing over to turn right up Purfield Drive and following it to the top. Here turn right (Blakes Road) for 50 yards and cross over to old metal swing-gate and follow footpath ahead. At top of field, cross footbridge and turn left along field-edge, with hedge on left.

1 At lane ahead (Highfield Road) turn left for 100 yards, then join path in field on right and follow wide grass strip round two sides. Turn right along road (Crazies Hill Road) and then 40 yards past drive entrance of Hennerton Golf Club turn left over stile. Stay close to hedge on left to reach stile in far left corner where path descends steeply to another stile, then crosses end of field. At bottom of valley turn right onto rising bridleway (Penny's Lane). *How many centuries did it take to carve out this ancient, sunken track, joining Crazies Hill to the Henley Road?*

2 Finally reaching road, immediately turn left between field-gates into footpath through wooded strip, with scattered cottages of Crazies Hill in view across field to right. Soon look out on left for glimpse of Summerfield House in its spacious grounds, with recently formed lake. *This elegant Georgian building served as Henley-on-Thames's Town Hall, overlooking the market place for nearly a century before being taken down in 1897 and re-erected here. It*

Rebecca's Well

obviously enjoys its retirement!

Emerging opposite Village Hall, turn right along road and where this dips down, bending right, go straight on into a gravel byway past Rebecca's (delightful) Cottage. Before entering footpath shortly on right, go ahead for 25 yards to view Rebecca's Well. *This spring used to be the hamlet's water supply. In 1870 the curate of Wargrave, Rev. Greville Phillimore invited subscriptions to build this pictorial well-head.*

Returning to footpath, follow it through copse and up to swing-gate at field-side. Head straight across to railed stile in far corner. When narrow path on roadside bank descends continue along lane until, just beyond the yard of Highfield Farm, cross stile beside gate on left and head up middle of field past line of oaks. At path junction at top of field go straight on, beside firs on left, before descending a stepped board-walk to footbridge over gulley (Bottom Boles Wood).

3 At grass field ahead turn right along one side before turning left into hedged byway known as Green Lane. Follow this track as far as end of field on right where a swing-gate marks a permitted path (see our map for alternative route) which shadows the copse then descends over open grassland to swing-gate. *See notice about path status under Countryside Access scheme - hopefully still available after 2007.*

4 Descend Hanover Gardens and turn right along footway leading around the estate of Highfield Park to reach Blakes Road. Here cross over, turning left for some 30 yards before turning right through two metal gates. A 'desire path' ahead, crosses field to reach gate into recreation ground and the well-tended greensward at start.

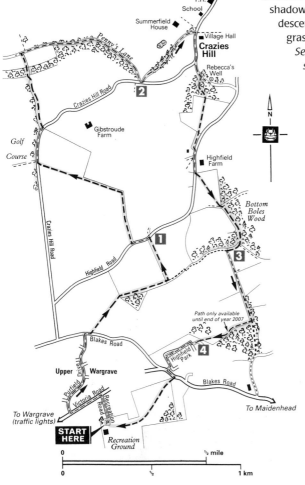

DATE WALKED

Ruscombe Church and Mumbery Hill

If you have an hour or so to spare – morning, noon or summer's evening, – this short walk on good paths across open farmland can be followed in either direction, the return by train taking just 4 minutes! (Usually an hourly service.)

As an alternative, to make a circular walk use Ramble 24 in **RAMBLING FOR PLEASURE AROUND READING (1ST Series)** as the first leg.

Distance: 3 miles
OS Map: Explorer 159 Reading
Start: Twyford Station
(or Wargrave Station).

Twyford Station to Wargrave
Leave station forecourt by path beside ticket office. Carefully cross road, turning right across bridge and at start of hedge turn left into playing-field (Stanlake Meadow). This Permitted Path follows the railway then swings right to stile by gate. Here turn left along tree-shaded lane, over railway, then bear right on slip-road just before crossroads. Keep turning right (into Church Lane) and walk between the trees towards St James the Great, Ruscombe.

In front of church bear left along lane and at crossroads carefully go over into Castle End Road. Within 100 yards fork left on bridleway, gravel at first, and shortly bear right in front of gates at Northbury Farm. *The group of listed buildings here includes the (just visible) timber-framed Elizabethan manor house of Northbury, sympathetically restored in 1988/89.* At end of field on right follow bridleway over New and London Roads, heading diagonally across open field to far right corner. In next field follow line of trees on grass strip, then ahead on gravel to the Bath Road (A4).

Carefully cross road, go through bridle-gate, and follow ascending track (passing Sheeplands Farm away to left). Reaching road (Mumbery Hill) turn left along footway until, just before first property on left, turn left (by seat) onto descending field-edge path. At first corner of field keep right, beside garden fences, with burial ground in one-time chalk pit below on right. Reaching unmade road cross to tree-lined path on right of Orchard End. At main road (A321) turn right, then shortly left, into Station Road, at the end of which is the station.

May Day celebrations at Ruscombe Church

From Wargrave Station to Twyford

Join footway bearing right into Station Road, passing at one point on left, the elegant war memorial by Edwin Lutyens on the Green (access here also to the Church, village landing stage and three pubs). At end of Station Road turn right and cross over. Shortly ahead turn left, in front of Leafy Lane House, into tree-lined rising path. Reaching unmade road either go straight ahead to view burial ground in old chalk pit or go a few paces right to go up, between concrete posts, into narrow path beside garden fences on right. At corner of field continue ahead leading up field-edge to road (Mumbery Hill). Here bear right along footway until, just before first house ahead on left, turn right into wide track leading down to Bath Road (A4).

Cross with great care, pass left of gate and straight on over gravel to follow line of trees ahead between fields. At corner of next field route follows diagonal line to far side. Here bridleway crosses London and New Roads and continues beside field now with hedge on right. This is an old way, as well as our way, to Ruscombe Church. *Notice on left along here path into small wood, 5 acres of one-time osier beds now cared for by FORWOOD - Friends of Ruscombe Wood.*

Reaching lane, facing pair of cottages, bear right and shortly cross into Church Lane. Either follow church fence bearing right or cut through the pretty churchyard. Follow lane, noticing Ruscombe Lodge (the vicarage in Victorian times), bearing left before crossroads. *Double hedge along here hides 'Penn's Garden', recalling William Penn, founder of Pennsylvania, who spent his last few years at nearby Ruscombe House (now demolished).*

Cross railway bridge and within 100 yards turn right over stile and cross playing-field to exit in right-hand corner. Turn right over railway bridge, then immediately left down tarmac path to station.

To Henley
R. Thames
St. Mary's Church
Greyhound P.H.
WARGRAVE
Wargrave Station
Cemetery
Seat & Viewpoint
Mumbery Lane
Sheeplands Farm
A4
London Road
Local Nature Reserve
Northbury Farm
Ruscombe
TWYFORD
START HERE
Twyford Station
St James Church
To Maidenhead
To Reading
Rec.
B3024
N

0 — ½ mile
0 — 1 km

Pitlands Farm and Weycock High-road

Share the view from Knowl Hill enjoyed by the Romans who once lived in this area. Follow the old tracks leading to Waltham St Lawrence, a Saxon village owned in 1006 by Ethelred the Unready. This is an easy, level walk but can be very muddy after wet periods so, unlike the King, do go suitably prepared!

Distance: 4¼ miles

OS Map: Explorer 159 Reading

Start: Lay-by near 'Seven Stars' on Bath Road (A4) at Knowl Hill. (Grid ref: 822 794)

With your back to 'Seven Stars' turn left along footway, passing Village Hall and use footbridge to cross A4. From school entrance walk forward 30 paces and turn left through wooden gate to cross corner of churchyard. Turn left up lane for 50 yards then bear half-right across grass strip to join well-used path up through trees to emerge at top of Common, with bench seat nearby and extensive views to Windsor Castle, Ascot racecourse and even on a clear day to the tower at Canary Wharf.

From seat take the clear path down hillside towards far left corner of Common. Cross road, go a few yards along drive, then turn right along edge of Common. Turn left along lane past house and buildings of Lower Lovetts Farm. At junction of three ways, take the stony, middle (Footpath) route. Go straight on past substation, becoming field-edge path, with hedge on right at first, later on left. At road (Bottle Lane) turn right. Where road turns left (notice this unusual cottage) go straight ahead into gravel drive of Pitlands Farm.

1 After house, path continues ahead on grass path. Pass between wooden posts and continue along field-edge beside hedge. After track joins from left, stay on field-edge until it swings right. Here go straight on, over railway footbridge. Continue on field-edge for some 200 yards, where a finger-post indicates path leaves headland, turning some 30 degrees across large field to stile in far corner, just left of large house (former Victorian vicarage). After this stile turn left, then shortly right into Halls Lane, leading down to village centre, perhaps taking path across

... leave headland to follow line indicated across large field

corner of churchyard to admire the incredible 17th century 'Wilkinson's Yew'. *The 14th century Bell Inn was given to the church in 1608 by Ralph Newbery, Lord of the Manor, who was Master Printer to Queen Elizabeth I.*

2 To continue the walk, turn right beyond lych-gate and cross stile beside gate to Church Farm. The right of way shortly bears right, passing in front of farmhouse, then threads its way between farm buildings to emerge on a broad track between open fields, with the twin peaks (!) of East Berkshire ahead, Bowsey to left, Ashley to right. Re-cross railway at bridge ahead.

In 1847 the field on left, known as Weycock Hill, was excavated to reveal the remains of an octagonal Roman temple, similar to one at Silchester. The temple here may have been an important religious centre for the many villas known to have existed in this area. At one time the way from London left the main road at the 29th milestone and ran across here to the village, being known as Weycock High-road.

3 Where track divides by solitary tree bear right, leading to stile to left of trees (Effie's Copse, named after the late Miss Effie Barker, an indefatigable local fox-hunter). Continue ahead on bridleway, conveniently shielded by hedges on both sides from wayward golf balls. Eventually track reaches a road. Turn right for a few paces, then climb steps up bank, go right on drive

and into narrow path between garages, leading to edge of Knowl Hill Common. Go ahead over two crossing drives, then continue on same line ahead over common, to trees on far side, beyond which hides white-painted Hope Cottage. Turn left along lane, past Royal Oak just ahead, leading back to A4 and the start.

DATE WALKED		

The Green Lanes of St Lawrence

Little has happened to alter the farms and fields round this old Saxon village since the vicar, Thomas Wilkinson, planted his yew tree in the churchyard in 1655 and in the same year Mabel Modwyn was 'arraigned for witchcraft and condemned'. Unusually, the church owns the village pub!

Distance: 5½ miles
OS Map: Explorer 159 Reading
Start: Waltham St Lawrence Parish Church, in centre of village. (Grid ref: 829 769)

With your back to church lych-gate (facing ancient pound) turn right along Milley Road. Taking due care of the traffic, pass houses at first, then open field on left. At end of this field bear left onto bridleway beside The Old Press. Follow track (Nut Lane) to finally emerge and turn right, crossing over, along wide verge (Twyford Road). Follow iron fencing to end of field on left and, opposite St Lawrence Orchard, turn left through metal swing-gate. Follow path-line through a series of these gates, at first along hard track beside fields, then on grass field-path, ending at stile beside gate and wooden shelter, next to a hedged track (Mire Lane).

1 Here turn right along track, soon becoming surfaced, passing West End Farm and, shortly, Viners. At road junction turn left, soon passing colour-washed former Plough inn. Bear right along Bailey's Lane for short distance, then at second drive turn right onto path beside timber-framed Bailey's Cottage. This hedged track leads to path junction facing open field. Cross this field to footbridge and go straight on for some 50 yards to another bridge. Now continue along edge of copse (bluebells in May!) with deep ditch on left, leading to road.

2 At road (Hungerford Lane) turn left for 80 yards, then cross stile on left and head across middle of field to gap on left side of trees on far side. Woodland path passes left of 'Goosenest' cottage and continues along gravel drive. At road turn right and just ahead, at junction with Brook

On the woodland path leading to Hungerford Lane

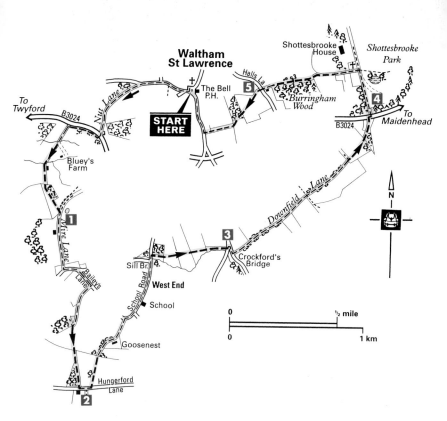

Lane, go straight on along footway of School Road, through the hamlet of West End.

Just beyond telephone box cross Sill Bridge and immediately turn right over stile by gate to join footpath, beside panelled fence at first, then straight on over three meadows, then behind handful of houses to reach road by Crockford's Bridge.

3 Cross ahead over both roads then turn right for 30 yards to join bridleway, Downfield Lane, on right-hand side of property. Follow this old green lane for about ¾ mile until finally, where track turns sharp left, cross stile ahead and bear slightly left through field to exit at metal field-gate and on along grass track. At roadside turn right, crossing over, to enter bridleway into Shottesbrooke Park.

4 Keep shallow ditch on left to reach drive ahead in front of medieval church of St John, beautifully kept and remarkably unaltered since it was built in 1337. Turn left through metal kissing-gate and follow flagstoned path past church porch and ahead between high brick walls. Path continues between field and ha-ha (a cunning device of fence in a man-made ditch to preserve an open view, in this case from Shottesbrooke House). At corner of wood ahead continue in next field along edge at first, then through trees to road (Halls Lane).

5 Cross straight over where path ahead follows series of wooden kissing-gates, finally through little-used allotment garden to road. Here turn right along footway of The Street, back through village to start.

DATE WALKED		

Stud Green and Blackbird Lane

This easy, level walk from the delightful old village of Holyport is through tranquil countryside ranging from lush meadows to trim polo grounds. It can be muddy after wet weather so do go suitably shod.

Distance: 4½ miles
OS Map: Explorer 160 Windsor
Start: War Memorial on Holyport Green. (Grid ref: 892 778)

With your back to the War Memorial, turn half-right over middle of Green and cross road to enter footpath slightly to left of white-painted house (formerly The Cricketers). After concrete footbridge follow right-hand side of field ahead (beware of boggy areas). From stile in corner take path forking left, keeping close to left-hand hedgerow through next two fields. In third field, keep following hedge until this turns sharp left. Here bear right across field to stile on far side. Path ahead goes over footbridge and then stile to follow left side of field. Approaching stables, keep to left of boarded fence along an unloved path, to emerge on roadway at Stud Green.

1 Here turn left and after a few properties turn right into Rolls Lane. Where track ends at gate ahead, turn left past wooden barrier into narrow footpath, soon with hedgerow and ditch on left. After stile into field, continue ahead beside hedgerow. In next field (currently a polo pitch), just beyond gateway into field on left, turn left through gap in hedge, to cross stile and take diagonal line through two fields to stile at road (A330) in far corner. Cross over road, turning right, towards Touchen End.

Immediately after The Poplars cottages turn left on concrete farm track, which soon swings left. Facing gateway to Foxley Court Farm, turn right along conifer-lined track with paddocks on right. Eventually, at end of conifers, turn right along track - Long Lane.

2 At isolated white-painted cottage go 35 yards beyond it and turn left over footbridge on grass path round two sides of paddock, then turn right,

The Green at Holyport

becoming field-edge, with hedge on right. At end of this field turn right, where marker post points way between open fields. Shortly, path turns left with deep ditch on left at first and continues to end of big field. Pass over footbridge and cross end of small field before turning left over white-railed bridge and along tree-lined bridleway - Blackbird Lane - where you may well hear one!

3 On reaching road (B3024), turn right for some 120 yards and directly after Old Beams Kennels, turn left into hedged track known as Primrose Lane. Follow this old way for nearly ½ mile until, about 200 yards beyond pond beside path, turn left and cross plank footbridge. Keep to right of field beside ditch at first, then join track to road (Moneyrow Green). Cross over into Bartletts Lane which continues as a tree-lined track. Reaching main road (A330) ahead, turn right on gravel path along edge of Holyport Green to return to start.

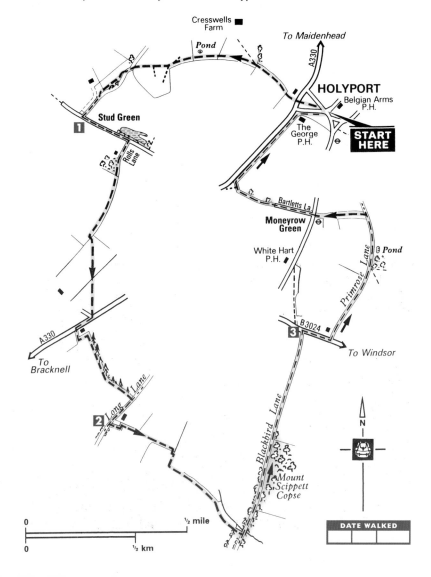

Fifield and Gays Lane

This wedge of surviving countryside in the historic parish of Bray is surprisingly thinly populated, giving a feeling of remoteness despite its nearness to Maidenhead and Windsor. The walk forms a double loop, linked together in Fifield village, offering an easy shorter alternative.

Distance: 3¾ or 5½ miles
OS Map: Explorer 160 Windsor
Start: War Memorial on Holyport Green. (Grid ref: 892 778)

Facing the War Memorial go ahead along Holyport Street past pond and Belgian Arms. At end of road cross stile and turn right through field to stile at roadside. Carefully cross over and head along Stroud Farm Road until, after last bungalow on left, turn into footpath, soon following avenue of conifers. Coming to an open area turn right beside fence and through to nearby swing-gate.

The rising ground ahead has been reclaimed after mineral extraction, enabling access to be re-opened on the original line of the right of way and now providing wide, open views from the higher ground.

1 From this point, keeping fenced hedgerow on right all the way, follow path straight ahead through several fields (some ¾ mile in fact), finally to emerge at roadside, beside small terrace of cottages. Here turn left along Coningsby Lane to T-junction just ahead. For the shorter walk turn right here through Fifield village, past 'Hare & Hounds' (see map).

2 To continue the longer walk turn left at T-junction (Fifield Road) until, beside last property on right, turn into a rough, hedged path. At end of enclosed strip turn left into field, then immediately right to continue ahead, keeping hedge on right around three sides of big field; finally to cross first footbridge in corner and *turn left* into hedged strip. At end of this strip turn right along field-edge for some 75 yards where path continues between hedges. At end of enclosed section turn

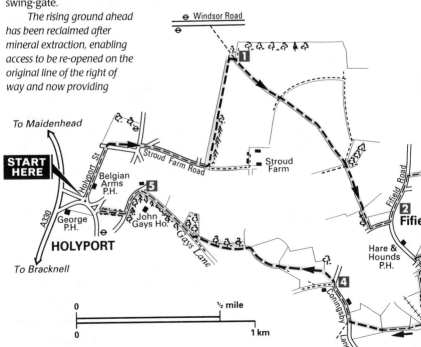

Coningsby Lane *Painting by John Manson*

right to cross open field and leave over culvert, to continue ahead along side of next field.

3 At T-junction of paths turn right and now, keeping hedge on left, walk through five fields (origin of Fifield?!) to emerge finally in village (where short walk rejoins - see map). Cross over, turning left along footway until, just beyond pair of houses turn right into rough drive. In front of

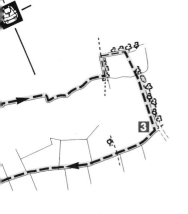

pillared gateway shortly ahead turn left into narrow wooded path. *The whole length of this path was impenetrable until 1971 when it was cleared by members of the then newly-formed East Berks group of the Ramblers' Association.*

Emerging at track, keep left then almost immediately turn right to cross stile into field. Path ahead leads beside paddocks until at road turn right (Coningsby Lane again) shortly passing house and barn.

4 Where road swings right, cross stile on footpath into field on left. Path runs ahead across middle of two fields, (to far corner of second), then beside left-hand hedge in the third. Cross pair of stiles by bridge over ditch into meadow, then pass left of cluster of oaks to stile in far corner. Turn right along well surfaced track, called Gays Lane.

5 Where track forks, keep left and turn left along road (Langworthy Lane) for about 150 yards. Almost opposite gateway of John Gay's House, turn right into footpath (known locally as the 'Click Clack' and reputedly haunted!) which leads back to Green at start.

DATE WALKED		

Hogoak Lane and Tickleback Row

Explore the wedge of unspoilt, quiet countryside still to be found between Maidenhead and Bracknell. Our circuit starts in Warfield, at St Michael's Church (one of Berkshire's finest) and strides on through fields and green lanes. The length of the walk can be reduced to 6 miles by a short cut via Hawthorn Hill (see map).

Distance: 8½ miles
OS Map: Explorer 160 Windsor
Start: Free car park opposite Warfield Church. (Grid ref: 880 723)

Leaving car park turn left along Church Lane to cross stile into first field on right, next to Vicarage. Go half-left over two paddocks to stile in hedge and continue on same line to footbridge in bottom corner. Here path has been diverted to follow line of stream on left, marked by metal 'rambler stileways'. Go up steps and turn left (over Wane Bridge) up lane, shortly turning right on path into field. Follow this clear path straight ahead, past farm buildings on left, until finally reaching road, by Brockhill Farm.

... then join track passing to right of stable

1 Turn left up footway, towards hamlet of Brockhill, before soon turning left along short concrete drive. Pass houses on right, then keep right on surfaced track at first, beside ditch and hedge. Look left along here for a glimpse of Warfield Church. Where surfaced track turns away, continue ahead, still beside hedge on right, finally to reach road. Cross ahead into Garson's Lane. Follow this quiet country road and just beyond bend by Whitelock's Farm turn left. *Here for shorter route, see map,* but to continue the full circuit, after white-painted cottage shortly ahead turn right into Hogoak Lane, a delightful tree-lined old byway which passes a BBONT nature reserve, Chawridge Bank.

2 Follow Hogoak Lane for more than a mile before reaching the Drift Road, a one-time drove road to London from the west. Here turn left, crossing over, and take hedged path on right, just past two modern houses (replacing a cider house). Reaching open field ahead, turn left through middle of field to stile. In next field cross ditch between white metal rails, join track ahead to find stile in hedge, just right of brick stable. Now cross bridleway and continue ahead on field-edge, dotted with splendid mature oaks marking the way, with a right-hand kink in second field. About 75 yards along headland of next field turn right at waymark post, and over stile, to head half-left across field towards stile on far side, just right of white-gabled house (Long Lane Farm).

3 At stile, immediately turn left along hedged bridleway. Reaching metalled road turn right, soon becoming grass track. After metal gate, keep along left side of field to swing-gate, followed by hedged path to road. With great care cross over into Sheepcote Lane, to take footpath before first property on left, the drive to 'Windmills' where, immediately left of house, cross stile in hedge and continue in same direction, now on surfaced path. After 'dog leg' to right carry on, soon passing through yard to road. Here cross over, turning right, and continue for a 100 yards to join a field-path at metal gate. *This path was opened as a Right of Way in 1998 following much research of old records by local Ramblers' Association stalwart, Robin Mosses.*

4 Path follows field-edges, with road on right at first, includes two right and left turns, but stays beside ditch until in final field ditch runs ahead into trees and path turns left, soon with open view of The Cut, a much more appealing stream than the name suggests! Exit field just before a ford, to join track straight on

ahead. *Footbridge to right over stream leads to nearby Westley Mill.* Follow hedged byway (Hazelwood Lane), pass caravan park and then go straight on as byway continues. Look for first house on left, behind hedge, and turn left along roadway through hamlet of Tickleback Row, emerging at crossroad by Shepherds House.

5 Cross ahead, past Moss End Farmhouse. Roadway shrinks to single track and we fork right, before turning left at start of brick wall. Keep left of yard and join metalled track. At a 'circus' of gates, go through left-hand pair, as footpath ahead leads round paddocks on right, shortly to return to car park at start.

DATE WALKED

To Maidenhead

A3024

Bridge House P.H.

Sheepcote Lane

A330

Long Lane Farm

3

Braywoodside

The Bourne

Drift Road

Drift Road

N

4

The Cut

Ford

Pendry's Lane

HAWTHORN HILL

Hawthorn Lane

Ashmore Lane

Hugoak Lane

Chawridge Bank (BBONT Nature Reserve)

2

Whitelock's Farm

Hazelwood Lane

Shepherds House P.H.

5

Tickleback Row

Buckle Lane

Moss End

Garson's Lane

A330

To Ascot

START HERE

P

Warfield

† Church

The Cut

Wane Bridge

B3022

Brock Hill

1

0   1 mile

0   1 km

To Bracknell Town Centre

Monks Alley and Orange Hill

Despite recent development Binfield still retains its own distinctive rural charm, seen best from the leafy 'green lanes' we follow, with so many interesting properties, new and old, large and small. The map shows two loops forming shorter alternative routes (not described in the text).

Distance: 4½ miles
O.S. Maps: Explorer 159 Reading and 160 Windsor & Bracknell
Start: Parking area at Wicks Green, accessed along gravel drive beside 65 Stevensons Drive, off Terrace Road North, Binfield. (Grid ref: 841 714)

Take path in left corner of parking area, cross bridge over ditch and follow surfaced path (over Silver Jubilee Field) to turn left along quiet lane, called Wicks Green. Shortly turn right into Monks Alley. After Angel Farm on right the lane shrinks to a leafy byway, leading to a T-junction. Here turn right onto steadily ascending track (Green Lane). Reaching top look across road

(Carter's Hill) offering 90 degree views towards Ashley and Bowsey Hills with Chiltern Hills in far distance.

1 Turn right up tree-lined road. Carefully negotiate bend past Billingbear Lane and follow wide verge beside high wall of Billingbear House. (Footpath leaving road beside East Lodge offers short-cut back to start.) Further ahead along road turn left at Grove Cottage along drive to Orange Hill.

2 Where tarmac finishes and drive swings right, take footpath tucked in hedge on left. Cross two fields with 'rambler stileways' each end (a feature of the countryside around Bracknell). Emerging on narrow lane, turn right, leading down to junction with busy B 3018. Here turn left for a few paces then cross over into hedged bridleway.

3 At the top of this lane turn right past the buildings of Hill Farm and along a straight tarmac drive (a public bridleway) emerging beside Stubbs Hill football ground, opposite cemetery. Turn right up hill and shortly continue ahead on footway leading to Binfield's 14th century parish church of All Saints,

Angel Farm *Painting by John Manson*

on the hillside. *The gravelled drive to car park beside church offers a glimpse of the splendid former Rectory.*

To continue walk, we recommend crossing road from outside 'Barngates', turning right along footway into Terrace Road North, soon passing 'Jack O'Newbury' *(a pub since 1730, named after a famous and wealthy cloth merchant in Henry VIII's time - 'a man of merry disposition and honest conversation!')*

4 Footway ascends and near top of slope cross carefully into Wicks Hill. Just beyond pair of modern houses set back from lane, bear right into field-edge strip and then turn left along second side of field to re-join road. Turn left for a few yards then right, through a swing-gate, to follow perimeter path to left, round Wick's Green open space, leading back to start.

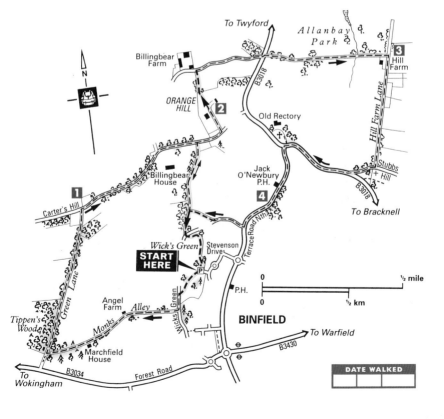

The Cut through Winkfield

An easy, level stroll through the lush green meadows still surrounding the historic centre of old Winkfield, with its medieval church and centuries-old coaching inn. Cross (twice) the diminutive Cut, a tiny stream reputedly home to the ubiquitous minnow and stickleback.

Distance: 3½ miles

OS Map: Explorer 160 Windsor & Bracknell

Start: Playing-field car park, junction of Forest Road/ Chavey Down Road, at Winkfield Row. (Grid ref: 897 711)

Leaving car park, turn right and follow footway past restaurant (formerly White Horse pub) and assortment of houses on right until, at end of wall to Grove Lodge, turn right into Grove Lane.

1 At end of lane, by white cottage, turn right through swing-gate into path beside meadow. Keep to this continuously fenced path (there is little choice!) through a series of so-called 'rambler stileways', leading beside the fields and over a stream (the Cut). At top of final field, faced with choice of ways, turn left along an old route called Parker's Lane, soon with ditch on right.

At wooden gate ahead, go straight on along narrow roadway, soon to turn right on gravelled footpath (just before Appletree Cottage). Shortly pass Millstone Cottage on left and go straight on along grass path, hedged both sides. Cross field ahead through swing-gates either end, then weave your way across garage forecourt, to cross road in front of the 'Drunken Pear', turning right along footway - Maiden's Green.

2 Where road soon forks, bear left along Winkfield Street, passing an assortment of village properties, including the Cottage Inn. Just beyond 'Old Timbers' turn right into narrow fenced path. Enter corner of field and within a few yards, by power-pole, join the path bisecting the meadow. After swing-gate into next field, follow fence on left at first, then keep right of solitary oak to reach stile beside metal gate. From this point head for church (12th century St Mary's, Winkfield) to find swing-gate into churchyard. Follow wall to road and cross over, turning left in front of pub.

Along the churchyard wall note the arched brick gateway to Old Rectory

A stop at Winkfield to refresh body and soul

House, built at same time as nearby church tower. The cost of the tower in 1639, replacing a wooden one, was £181 2s 10 1/2d. If open, do view inside of church where the roofs are supported by five oaks dated 1592. See also recent Wild Life and Millennium windows. The White Hart Inn was originally the manorial court-house of Winkfield, becoming a coaching inn in the more recent past.

3 From the White Hart follow footway until, at end of wooden fence, beside tall iron gates, turn right into grass footpath, soon with hedges and fields both sides. Entering field ahead follow hedgerow trees on left and at bottom corner cross sleeper-bridge. Emerging at roadside (Braziers Lane) turn right, using verge if possible until, some 20 yards past bridge (Coopers Bridge over the Cut), turn right through swing-

gate, joining Ramblers' Route as it goes round two sides of large field before turning right. Cross ends of two fields, then continue along fenced track, finally to reach stile by gate. Here note the unusual carved stone heads, high on the end wall of Hollington House. Now turn left, completing our circuit. Retrace your steps along Grove Lane, turning left along Chavey Down Road and so back to car park at start.

We can see gables
the lawn with tables
the barn and stables
of the old White Hart,
the car wheels crunching
the people lunching
drinking, and munching
their apple tart.

An extract from 'The view from the tower' by Simon Baynes, former Vicar of Winkfield.

DATE WALKED		

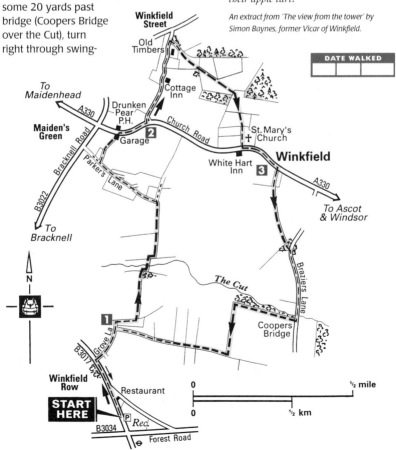

To many people, **Ascot** means hats, or horses! But not everyday. While this is an opportunity to walk across the world famous racecourse instigated in 1711 by that sporting monarch Queen Anne, it is also a chance to wander through woods and by the huge lake in **Sunninghill Park**.

Distance: 6 miles

OS Map: Explorer 160 Windsor

Start: Shops and bus stops in New Road, Brookside, North Ascot. (Grid ref: 919 707) See map for alternatives.

With your back to pillar box turn left along footway of New Road. At road junction cross and turn left (Forest Road) along footway until reaching drive entrances on both sides of road. Cross over to join footpath at wrought iron pedestrian gate, along drive of Mill Ride Golf Club. *This is an old coach road from an historic property nearby, Ascot Place.*

1 Part way along drive, opposite entrance to stud farm, turn left along hard track, soon becoming roadway and passing school. At mini-roundabout continue ahead and where footway ends, go on for 20 yards on grass verge before forking right into narrow fenced path. Emerging at road cross over, turning right, joining tarmac path beside Kennel Avenue. In front of Huntsman's House turn left, along avenue of stately Wellingtonias. *Queen Anne's Buckhounds were kennelled near here. You are now following, in reverse direction, a short section of the THREE CASTLES PATH, the 60-mile long distance route from Windsor to Winchester, devised and first published by East Berks Ramblers' Group in 1992 and now shown on current OS Explorer maps.*

2 At end of Kennel Avenue carefully cross main road and go straight ahead across racecourse. *If racing is in progress you may be held up for a few minutes but there is free public access to Ascot Heath even on race days.* With care continue ahead over golf course to join roadway passing cricket ground. At T-junction of roads turn right, now with racecourse on left. Where course turns right towards stands turn left across it. Pass to right of clubhouse and turn right along road. This crosses two sections of the course, after which our route turns left, into tree-lined path (by 30 mph sign) and leads to the Golden Gates.

These gates and adjoining lodge (a listed building) were erected in 1879 at the start of the original straight mile course.

Late spring morning on the old Coach Road

CULDN'T COMPLETE WALK DUE TO FOOT + MOUTH RESTRICTION

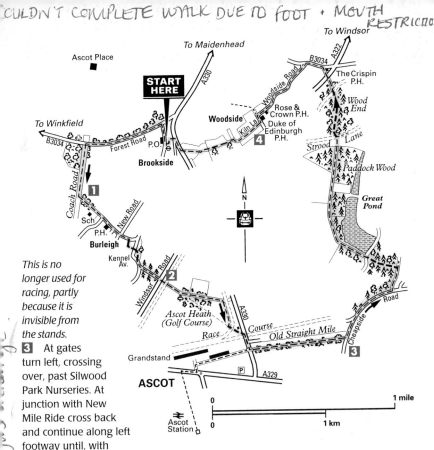

To Maidenhead

Ascot Place

START HERE

To Winkfield

Forest Road

P.O.

Brookside

Woodside

Kiln La.

Rose & Crown P.H.

Duke of Edinburgh P.H.

4

To Windsor

The Crispin P.H.

Wood End

Woodside Road

Strood Lane

Paddock Wood

Great Pond

1

Coach Road

New Road

Sch

P.H.

Burleigh

Kennel Av.

Windsor Road

2

Ascot Heath (Golf Course)

Race Course

Old Straight Mile

Cheapside Road

3

This is no longer used for racing, partly because it is invisible from the stands.

3   At gates turn left, crossing over, past Silwood Park Nurseries. At junction with New Mile Ride cross back and continue along left footway until, with

Grandstand

ASCOT

Ascot Station

P

A329

0   1 mile

0   1 km

N

Watersplash Lane just ahead, turn into drive past dinky thatched East Lodge (Sunninghill Park). At bottom of curving slope of drive turn left along winding woodland path, over a footbridge, cross a track and go ahead on wide track, concrete at first, beside Great Pond.

Continue on this track until finally it plunges into the gloom of Paddock Wood and stops abruptly facing field at stile by gate. Go straight across meadow where 'rambler stileways' show the way across Strood Lane (an old road) and on through trees of Wood End. Cross riding track, pass right of cottages and over road just ahead, to turn right towards The Crispin. Before pub, turn left down track behind it and left again at road ahead (B3034), then take first turning left, with pointer on tree to Woodside. After blind bend

in road followed by several big properties, pass the diminutive 'Rose & Crown', turn left by the nearby 'Duke of Edinburgh', all part of the hamlet of Woodside.

4   A few yards beyond the 'Duke' turn right into rough track labelled Kiln Lane. *Despite its name, one householder appears to 'fire' concrete balls rather than pots!* At end of houses path turns right then left, over stile into gated track. Path narrows beside hedgerow trees/ditch on left, leading to swing-gate and stile into field. After another swing-gate in hedge follow right-hand side of paddocks to emerge at roadside. Now turn right and cross over. At Kennel Ride shortly ahead, enter narrow fenced path beside No. 1 Winkfield Road which leads back to start.

DATE WALKED		

Virginia Water and Coworth Park

From the sylvan glades of Windsor Great Park, the impeccable perfection of Coworth Park, to the majestic mansions of Wentworth. Definitely a walk with a wow! factor; not really rural, more Ruritania!

Note: Walkers using the public paths across Wentworth Golf Course should be prepared for slight delays when major tournaments are being played.

Distance: 7 miles
OS Map: Explorer 160 Windsor & Bracknell
Start: Ascot Station. Frequent trains back from Sunningdale Station take 5 minutes!

With your back to main station buildings head left towards footpath signed to Racecourse but at bottom of steps turn sharp left to pass through tunnel under railway. Walk down slope and bear right into All Souls Road, passing church. Where road swings left, fork off right into narrow woodland footpath. Reaching main road (A330) cross over, turning right, to end of railing and turn left on path beneath canopy of trees.

1 Emerging at road (Sunninghill) turn right along footway until, shortly beyond railway bridge, turn left into Coombe Lane, passing Tom Green's Field (see companion guide *THREE CASTLES PATH*). At end of this unsurfaced track carefully cross main road with aid of mirror! Turn right for a few yards, then left into painfully narrow path beside Wellsbridge Cottage.

2 At T-junction turn right, leading up to St Michael's Church. *The remarkable hollow yew tree here with its iron girdle is thought to be over 1,000 years old.* Cross churchyard on right, with its ornate monuments and join lane past burial ground. Go through kissing-gate and along grass strip between fields (known as Church Path). After another iron gate follow winding path, keeping iron fence (of Silwood Park) close on right.

Virginia Water

Emerging (Buckhurst Road) cross over turning right along footway and shortly bear left into Mill Lane and follow this (hopefully) quiet road, fringing Windsor Great Park, to Blacknest Gate. Here turn into park and immediately fork right across grass towards trees, to join tarmac drive. Shortly ahead turn left along lakeside path. Just beyond end of tall trees on left, with view of stone bridge back to left, turn away from lake up path through trees leading to large parking area. Cross to road exit and turn left (A329). Just after large Blacknest Gate sign cross road and face traffic until, at top of slope turn right, signposted Shrubs Hill.

3 Go straight ahead on drive (Bridleway) with views across polo ground to right. *These beautifully kept grounds with a wonderful assortment of architecture both old and new is Coworth Park, reputedly owned by the Sultan of Brunei.* Where drive finishes continue ahead through woodland to main road. Here turn left up footway (London Road). At top of hill cross carefully into West Drive, signed as footpath to Knowle Hill. Follow roadway between palatial properties of Wentworth estate.

After crossing one fairway of the course (15th) continue to next open area (large 'SS' on gates nearby). Here turn right onto wide gravel track. Shortly cross another fairway as right of way continues, now with course nearby through trees on right. Where track forks bear left and at next junction turn right, as track dips down over another fairway, then levels out through a wood until course appears again, on right. When level with a green (12th) turn left over small wooden bridge, then immediately right, away from fenced enclosure.

4 Follow narrow path through light woodland to join road with high hedges concealing houses both sides. Bear left at junction (Heather Drive), turn left (Onslow Road) and shortly cross over (Cobham Road), turning right *for only a few paces* before turning sharp left into narrow tarmac path. Keep straight on over two crossing tracks, soon with houses both sides. At road ahead follow it to left, to find main road at end of Halfpenny Lane(!). Here turn left along A30 shortly to reach Sunningdale Station.

DATE WALKED		

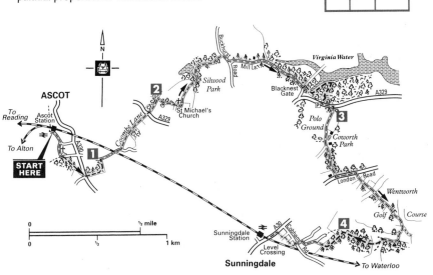

Lily Hill and Swinley Park

Despite the enormous population growth of Bracknell, from 3,000 in 1950 to over 50,000 today, it is still possible to follow a largely 'green' route visiting interesting wildlife sites and a historic hunting forest within a stone's throw of the town.

Distance: 5 miles
OS Map: Explorer 160 Windsor & Bracknell
Start: **A.** Car park at Longhill Park, Bullbrook, Bracknell. (Grid ref: 893 693)
Start: **B.** Alternatively, follow the same circuit, starting from Martin's Heron rail station.

Start A: With your back to the road, pass beside metal gate and go straight ahead across park on gravel path. Where path turns left, turn right and walk over the grass, round right side of overgrown dell, to leave corner of park down steps. Go ahead, between wooden rails, along cul-de-sac (Timline Green) and turn left up Badgers Way. Cross ahead, over Lily Hill Road and straight up bank into woods of Lily Hill Park.

This is one of Bracknell's many Wildlife Heritage Sites. Its 67 acres comprise mixed woodland and parkland. There are some 55 different tree species here which you may like to study more closely another time.

1 Climb to top of slope (Foresters Hill) to find near a bench a waymark post marked 'B'. Now bear left to follow the lettered 'tree trail', noticing the labelled specimen trees, many planted in the 1850s. At post after waymark 'F' disregard arrow and go *straight on*, down to roadside (London Road). Cross at traffic lights and head along Allsmoor Lane, an old road with a new surface, giving access to The Cottage. Round the corner here, turn sharp left after rail arch and follow tarmac path to Martin's Heron Station. Admire the superb 'graffiti' - along the right lines for a change!

There are different theories about the origin of this unusual name but in recent times it related to an estate in this area. Its Georgian mansion was demolished in 1983 to make way for new housing.

Passing Matravers' masterpiece!

Start B: From Platform 2 descend railed slope and turn left, to join tarmac path to end of wooden fence and turn right. At children's play-area turn left (stay on path) and at T-junction turn right onto driveway. Shortly ahead on left pass through metal swing-gate into the shady glades of Swinley Park, part of historic Windsor Forest. *For further details of this area see the THREE CASTLES PATH, another guide in our Rambling for Pleasure series.*

2 From this gate go ahead along broad ride. Just after first crossing ride, turn left, leading to a 'star' junction. Take the second 'spoke' from *left*. At next junction of rides take the second exit on *right* where waymark arrow points the way to exit park at swing-gate. Cross road, turning left to face traffic and beyond rail bridge, immediately cross fence on right into Nature Reserve. Shortly ahead, at path crossing (car park to left), turn right and follow lettered waymark posts of Nature Trail as it circles to left through what has become rare heathland.

3 At a point facing Englemere Pond (an ancient natural feature, now an SSSI) turn left on track crossing several small bridges, then at T-junction turn right along path known as Butterfly Ride. Shortly ahead the Nature Trail turns left into trees. From waymark 'G' take path bearing right, to pass corner of nearby building (timber yard) leading to London Road (A329).

Cross over at traffic lights, turning left along footway. Try to think beautiful thoughts (winning the Lottery perhaps!) and close your ears to the cacophony of sound along here. Pass the modern buildings of the Licensed Victuallers School and the older Royal Foresters Inn.

4 Cross Priory Road and at end of brick wall turn right up bank, on a right of way, through a woodland strip. This humble path stays near to fenced green bank, goes round two left-hand bends, finally to emerge at roadside, opposite our starting point.

DATE WALKED		

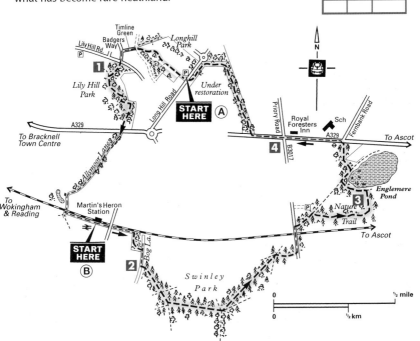

Round Hill and Caesar's Camp

Enjoy this most varied walk, embracing the wide open spaces of Bramshill Forest, the fascinating remains of an Iron Age hill fort and the elegant 18th-century landscape of Easthampstead Park. Can you ask for more?

Distance:	7 miles
OS Map:	Explorer 160 Windsor & Bracknell
Start:	**A.** Lay-by off Nine Mile Ride, opposite St Sebastian's Memorial Hall, Crowthorne. (Grid ref: 832 655)
Start:	**B.** Car park at Great Hollands recreation ground, South Road, Bracknell. (Grid ref: 852 665)

Start A: With your back to Honey Hill, go half-left into narrow gravel byway with fences on left, soon becoming roadway (Hatch Ride). Follow road to far end (admiring, or otherwise, the changing pattern of domestic architecture over the past fifty years!) At junction, turn right along busy road,

Crowthorne Wood bridleway

opposite grounds of Road Research Laboratory. Look out for first turning on left, Brookers Row. Here cross over and immediately turn right into an isolated section of Bramshill Forest. Within 50 yards turn left along wide grass ride. Take second track on left, back to roadside, crossing over and turning right along footway.

1 With great care cross road ahead (Bracknell Road) and leaving behind the cacophony of Crowthorne, stride straight ahead along a modest path into another part of Forestry Commission's Bramshill Forest (Crowthorne Woods), soon beside tall pines. Shortly turn left onto broad rising forest track. At prominent meeting of ways (top of Round Hill) take the bridleway bearing half-right, through trees at first, then rising more steeply, up to another crossing. Here go a few feet left before continuing on same line, on a minor path through trees, shortly dropping down steeply to the historic track known as the Devil's Highway. *This is the route of a Roman road from Silchester to London.*

Turn left along the 'Highway'. Shortly ahead, modern man has made his mark by bridging the Roman way. Just after passing under bridge, disregard wire-fenced footpath, but turn left to climb winding path up tree-covered slope. On the top it straightens out, with young trees on right. At first crossing path, bear right along prominent track. At next crossing, take path straight ahead (between trees) which curves left. Meeting a very prominent crossing turn right (with footpath sign). At next junction of rides, go on between wooden posts. Where avenue of trees ends go ahead and cross stile into southern entrance of Caesar's Camp.

2 Follow wide track ahead through middle of camp, at one point passing just left of tree-cloaked steep bank and ditch. Our way descends Queen Anne Gully (cut through the ramparts in

1702), swinging left at bottom to cross stile by metal gate. A few yards before another gate, turn left onto path in trees with road close by on right. Follow this path for a distance, finally crossing road to join start of metalled footway on the other side. At roundabout cross Crowthorne Road and continue to end of footway. Here turn right into woodland strip. Keep left of houses ahead and shortly bear left along broad avenue of trees with rhododendrons at their feet. Cross over (South Road) and turn right on path beside road.

Start B: From car park cross road to footway, turning right.

3 Pass cemetery and continue on verge beside tall conifers. At T-junction bear right, to follow golf course boundary fence until it turns left, where path becomes a wide footway. Pass school and enter drive, gated both ends.

Now take right fork in road ahead and shortly, where this bears right, go *straight ahead* between posts. Path now follows field edge beside tree-lined ditch.

4 At T-junction turn left, go straight across splendid tree-lined main drive of Easthampstead Park. Ahead soon join wide tarmac drive (part of Ramblers Route) leading to road. Here carefully cross over, turn right for 30 yards, then left over stile to another on far side of field. Turn right along road (Easthampstead Road) for about 250 yards before turning left at swing-gate. Head diagonally across two fields (with stile between) to footbridge in far corner. Go straight across next field to another bridge. Waymarked track ahead loops round past Honey Hill Cottage and at road turn left along Honey Hill back to start.

DATE WALKED		

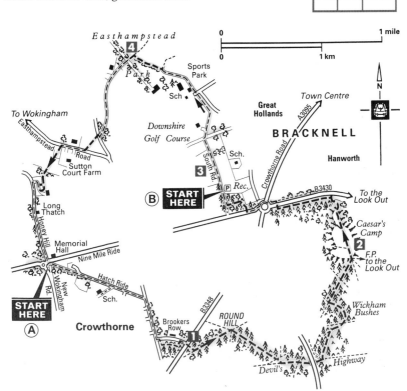

Chapel Green and Luckley Path

How wonderful it is to be able to walk from the centre of Wokingham to open countryside within a few minutes. The railways east and south of the town have acted as a buffer in holding back the tide of development. This gentle stroll explores a green corridor with barely a sign of habitation. Wander while you may!

Distance: 4½ miles
OS Map: Explorer 159 Reading
Start: Wokingham Library, off Denmark Street. (Grid ref: 811 683) See map for link with station.

Admire 'Waterbabies' sculpture at main entrance to library, then turn left down slope and left again on footway of Denmark Street. At mini-roundabout cross over, pass Dukes Head, then straight on down Finchampstead Road towards, and under, railway bridge. Just before next roundabout turn into footpath by two houses on left. After metal swing-gate follow gravelled track. At parking area go half-right up between paddocks to pass Chapel Green Farm followed shortly by Lucas Hospital.

1 *This splendid building of 1665 is owned by the Drapers Company and is the only Grade 1 listed building in Wokingham.* Admire the house from the main gate and then cross stile in corner, go round clump of holly and head across small meadow to leave by swing gate near right-hand corner. Turn right along tarmac drive (leading away from nearby Ludgrove School - a preparatory school whose 'old boys' include Princes William and Harry). A few strides beyond white pillars turn left beside metal gates into footpath, posing here as a wide gravel track which reveals occasional glimpses of the hospital back across the fields. After some distance the track swings left, away from the Wokingham/ Guildford railway, shortly to pass gate before property on right, known as Gorrick Cottage.

2 After cottage take first on right, by gate, becoming a wide track, soon through an open area. *It is easy to visualise the once tree-less heath that existed here before the land was enclosed in 1817. Today it is managed by the Forestry Commission.* Eventually track bears left and, shortly, left again at junction. Some 75 yards after this second bend, bear left into path through trees. Keep

'The Waterbabies' – our start point outside Wokingham Library

straight on, ignoring path off to left, until emerging from trees. Continue ahead now on broad gravel track (a line we shall follow for more than a mile back to Wokingham). Keep straight on over two prominent crossing tracks, followed by wooden footbridge, to an open ditch marking end of woodland.

3 Now continue between open fields at first. Path then narrows between fences, becoming grassy. Look out for sports field on left and at its end, with gate just ahead, fork left into narrow path with field on left. At metal swing-gate cross drive (to Ludgrove School). *The route we are following is known as Luckley Path and has existed for over 500 years. Notice shortly ahead small bridge over the diminutive Emm Brook, a reminder of the many tanneries which stood on its banks when leather was a major industry in the town.*

The path ahead rises and crosses footbridge over railway (Reading/Waterloo line). Turn left along road (Gipsy Lane) for some 50 yards, then turn right on path beside row of lime trees, *marking the only remaining part of one-time Langborough common field.*

4 Cross ahead at start of Howard Road, then keep straight on along fenced path before turning left through the attractive Howard Palmer Gardens (recalling a member of the Reading biscuit-making family).

Leaving Park, cross car park. To return to library, turn left down narrow walled path (Cockpit Path) and across lower parking area. If returning to station, do not turn left but go straight ahead, leading to Market Place and Town Hall (see map).

DATE WALKED

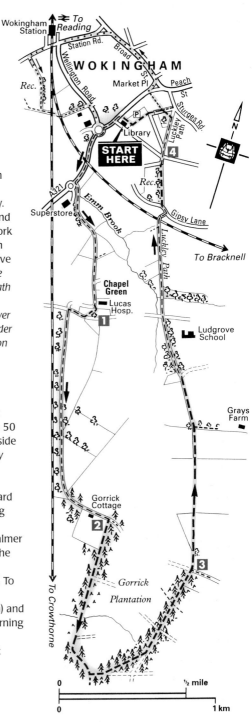

Woodcray Manor and Sand Martins

Many ramblers are also keen golfers. Here is an opportunity for them to see two courses from another perspective and, for those of a nervous disposition, at a safe distance. The former Evendon's Farm and Woodcray Manor Farm may have lost their rural identities but now sustain the sporting ambitions of a different herd!

NOTE: The route around Woodcray Manor Golf Course is useable but awaits erection of footpath signs and publication by Wokingham District Council of a Path Creation Order.

Distance: 4½ miles
OS Map: Explorer 159 Reading
Start: Car park off Evendons Lane, adjoining Redlands Farm Park. (Grid ref: 797 668)

From car park, carefully cross Evendons Lane into narrow footpath opposite. At path junction ahead, fork left for a few paces, then immediately turn left into tree-lined track, with golf course (Sand Martins) on both sides. Reaching T-junction, turn right, pass play-area and continue along narrow fenced path behind gardens. After metal barrier keep right, still along narrow fenced path, to emerge at Finchampstead Road (A321).

1 Carefully cross over, turning left along footway. A few yards after main entrance of Woodcray Manor Golf Course, turn right between concrete posts: the one-time farm drive. At *second* opening on left, turn left into broad gravel hedged track. Reaching a grass-covered mound, follow this until it levels out. Ahead turn right, to join winding path in woodland strip, with golf course on right and railway nearby on left. Emerging from trees at one point, path continues on low ridge, still beside course but now moving away from railway.

2 Emerging at bend in gravel drive, turn right. When a property appears ahead (Woodcray Cottage), look out for footpath turning sharp left off drive. Follow this modest path through woodland, now with course on left until, facing wooden gate, pass left of it and follow line of pines, soon to cross road ahead. Follow Tintagel Road and at the end (Kiln Ride) turn left, then

Sand Martins Golf Course from one of the new paths

immediately right, into and along Foxcote until, opposite No. 114, turn right into byway. Reaching Finchampstead Road (again) turn right, crossing over and follow footway to enter footpath beside entrance to Sand Martins Golf Course.

3 This railed path turns sharp right, now with pleasant views over the course towards the distant club house (once Evendon's farmhouse). Notice prominent sand hills, which attract nesting martins in the spring and give the course its name. Ignore footpath on right after garage enclosure and continue beside course until path runs beside drive. Notice the black-boarded former farm granary (the staddle stones were to deter rats getting to the grain). Shortly, turn left across 'zebra' and pass in front of clubhouse - where a sand martin is always wheeling around!

Footpath now follows broad track down slope and soon, near driving range, turns left, with course over fence on left and on right the Moors. This is a remnant of undrained wet woodland, now a nature reserve, a rare survivor surrounded as it is today by manicured greens and fairways.

4 At metal footbridge turn right (Waverley Way) for about 130 yards before bearing right along firm sandy path on bank, above ditch on right. Where firm path turns away, go straight on along wide grass ride, still beside ditch and trees. Reaching a metal railed footbridge over the ditch, turn right across it, to join the golf course perimeter path, leading back to path junction, thus completing our circuit. Here turn left, back to nearby Evendons Lane and car park.

DATE WALKED		

Wick Hill and Longwater Lane

A wonderful variety of woodland and river valley scenery all within the parish of Finchampstead. Explore the National Trust protected slopes of The Ridges and visit the Saxon hilltop church of St James.

Distance: 6½ miles

OS Map: Explorer 159 Reading

Start: Car park behind shops by double mini-roundabouts at junction of Finchampstead Road (B3016) and Nine Mile Ride, south of Wokingham. (Grid ref: 797 647)

Leaving car park turn right, then right again along Nine Mile Ride. Shortly fork right into gravelled Wick Hill Lane which steadily rises. At top of rise take left fork. Path ahead narrows, then widens again, before bearing right past large modern houses. Surfaced drive becomes rough track and continues through light woodland until emerging by cluster of properties. Notice Tudor Cottage - 'Beware of Cats'!

1 Follow drive (passing Wick Hill House) until at junction cross into Dell Road and descend, with some pleasant views on a clear day. Look out on left

Enjoy the view from this rising field-edge path

for an unusually large holly tree. Almost at bottom of slope take footpath on left beside Warren Cottage. At end of garden look out for small stone engraved '1913' marking start of NT Finchampstead Ridges. *The Ridges is one of the Trust's earliest acquisitions, the first 60 acres having been purchased by public subscription for £3,000, part of the Bearwood Estate owned by the Walter family, one-time owners of* The Times *newspaper.*

2 To ensure correct route, from the engraved stone count 175 (!) good strides, straight up path to a junction. (Two steeply ascending paths visable ahead.) Here take the path turning right at 90 degrees, to follow a well-used route, beside narrow ditch on left at first, staying roughly on the same contour of the hill. At first crossing path go straight on, then at second junction go ahead again, passing left of NT sign saying 'No Horses'. Path ahead, now with ditches both sides, soon starts bearing right, beside fence and bushes, leading to exit from NT woodland. Turn right down track, passing The Old Thatch, to reach and turn right along a quiet lane, Lower Sandhurst Road.

3 Reaching car park, turn left to join footpath beside lake leading to Blackwater River, county boundary with Hampshire. Turn right, over small footbridge, and along riverbank for a distance. At end of fields on right, fork right where path swings away to road (Longwater Road) at swing-gate. Cross over into field opposite, turning left along narrow ribbon of a gravel path as it winds round two sides of field close to ditch, to arrive at swing-gate and footbridge. Here turn right up hedged path between fields (Longwater Lane). At start of houses, to continue walk turn left, but first go ahead for about 20 paces to post on left where a plaque gives details of an incident involving King Henry VII back in 1501.

Retracing your steps, follow climbing path with fence on right, to emerge at road called The Village (B3348).

4 Turn right past garage and cross over road, shortly to enter playing-field gates near phone box. Take a line half-right, to pass play-area, towards top left corner of field and join adjacent hedged track. Follow this up to reach, after swing-gate and several steps, the Saxon parish church of St James on its man-made mound. Pass left of church and down path to gate.

Notice immediately on left plaque in wall to George V and nearby red oak. Ahead on the green is an oak marking Queen Victoria's first 50 years on the throne (see stone in bush) and across road on right is another, marking her death in 1901. At that time the pub here changed its name from White Horse to Queen's Oak, and now claims to be *the only one of that name in the country.*

5 Pass in front of the pub and on along road (Church Lane). Just beyond Church Farm Bungalow turn left at swing-gate on diagonal line across field to road. Cross carefully, turning left, then immediately right, through another wooden gate. Enjoy this open, rising, field-edge path with its fine view looking back towards the church and after further swing-gate soon reach junction which completes our circuit. Here turn left down Wick Hill and retrace your steps back to start.

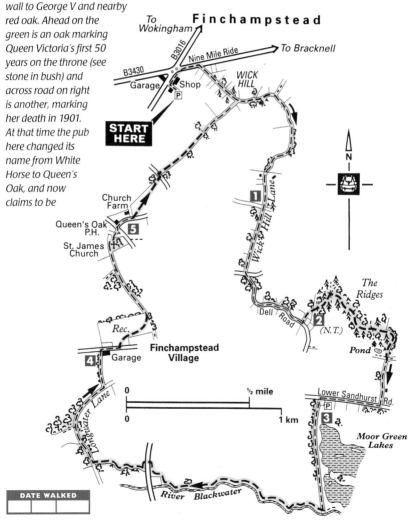

Ambarrow Hill and Finchampstead Ridges

A chance to sample some of the surviving areas of traditional heathland, managed today by the National Trust, around the beautiful and popular Finchampstead Ridges. Explore the slopes of Ambarrow Hill or perhaps picnic in the adjoining Country Park.

Distance: 4 miles
OS Map: Explorer 159 Reading
Start: Crowthorne Station.
(Grid ref: 823 638)

With your back to the main station buildings turn right along footpath, passing modern offices, soon with woodland on left. Reaching embankment of bridge (over railway) ahead, bear left and shortly turn right, to follow fenced path beside sports field (part of Bracknell's Ramblers' Route). Just after entering woodland ahead, turn right through metal swing-gate to cross railway, into NT 11 acre pine-clad woodland of Ambarrow Hill. *Is this cone-shaped hill a natural feature or could it be man-made? Nobody seems to know!*

1 Fifty yards ahead there are three choices: 1. To turn left into the grounds of one-time Victorian mansion, Ambarrow Court, now a country park. 2. Bear right to climb and explore Ambarrow Hill. 3. To continue walk, by staying on path ahead between holly bushes at first, along foot of hill until, just before road ahead turn left, signed 'Ambarrow Court', leading to car park. Here carefully cross road (A321) and pass via stileway along edge of woodland strip. Continue ahead along lane until, just past drive on right to Ambarrow Lodge, turn right on track through wood towards Bluebell Farm.

2 At green field-gate keep right, on path along edge of wood, with meadow sweeping up on left to the

Heath Pond